I wandered lonely in a
crowd
[a poetic panoply of
purgatory]

Smudge

Published by New Generation Publishing in 2021

Copyright © Smudge 2021

First Edition

ISBN   978-1-80369-157-2

Front cover image, courtesy of Jeffrey Czum
Back cover image, courtesy of Diane Simmonds

www.newgeneration-publishing.com

New Generation Publishing

Contents

Speak through me oh muse,

For I have nothing to say...

Homer

For Thomas Brannan

a good and gifted man

...sadly missed...

Acknowledgments

Firstly, to my Mother and Father, Annie and Tommy
Who coupled in a most fine and remarkable way,
 for their love, nurturing and guidance.

And then, my beautiful wife, Diane, for her continued
belief in me and for picking me up, when I would have
much rather been left in a heap, (also a damn fine cook and
homemaker).

My son. Lee Drew, for the late-night chats, the chess, his innate wise counsel, and his inbuilt navigation skills, a most excellent travelling companion.

My Daughter Lauren (Lozziepop), for encouraging me to write, when I had no words, a walking lexicon, humble, proud, awesome! Without whose help this work would have surely been filed under...maybe later, maybe not!

Finally, to the staff at New Generation Publishing, David and Daniel for their professional approach and good humour. Not forgetting Saskia, for her prompt replies to my rambling, often confusing emails, her patience, and guidance, without who's help this 'tome' would have never made it into print...
Thank you all
smudge

Foreword:

My first introduction to poetry, was in the form of my English teacher, I`ll call him Mister D. Formidable, humourless, positively terrifying. He would read out passages and explain the words, a brilliant etymologist.

And so, our task for a Monday evening, was to learn certain poems, all the classics and, recite them, in front of the class, on the Tuesday. I remember my first attempt, it came to my turn- my mind went blank, blind panic set in...

So, I learned a trick, a ' cheat', if you will if I could learn the poem in question by Seven O'clock, I get to watch Star Trek!

Therein developed a love-hate relationship.

As time went by, I heartily embraced the new-age movement but there were so many questions left unanswered.

Came the spring of 2018, attempting to make sense of it all, I wrote a verse, which languished in a notebook for a further six months.

One Saturday afternoon, I committed to finish- to scratch the `itch`, so to speak. I did indeed complete lo`, Distractions was born. And then another and, another. I wrote like a man possessed; the Muse came calling.

Another Saturday, sitting in a bar, or rather out in the smoking area, a passing comment from a stranger...The Regiment.. and on and on...

My Muse blessed me, sharing many ideas, which I in turn, would like to share with you...

Part One: Anthroposophy
(a study of spirit...)

Distractions

I wander'd with the Runes transfix't'
Until I turn'd my head,
The pendulum was callin' me
"Come with me", she said.

The Tarot cards were waitin'
Waitin' for to pounce,
"You've done a lot of work", they said,
Proudly to announce.

I go around in circles
Along this crook'd path,
Comin' to a crossroads,
"Whych way to go", I ask

On and on the path, she leads,
-then I found some Mala Beads!

Chantin' Swingin' Shufflin,
I'm in a state of flux,
"Gyide me I implore you
I havent' had much luck!"

Cards, Beads, Crystal,Stone,
And on and on it goes
Where's this journey
Leadin' us?
Noe one really knows

The Isle Of Avalon

As we gaze upon the Tor
What secrets lie within?
The darkest one that I recall...
The Abbot got done in!

Dissolution came to pass
Is where the story led
The portly king, upon the throne
Young Annie, he would wed

He wrote a letter to the Pope
Outlining his desires
A curt reply came winging back,
It's you I do despise!

The king was in a quandary
" I will not stand for this
The Pontiff, he will eat his words,
The man, he takes the pysse"

So, the story, to cut short
The King, he got his way,
Anne Boleyn, he did wed,
He found another way.

Many years before that,
On another day,
A young man named Joseph,
Would leave, without delay

Without hesitation,
Or procrastination
He set sail for Avalon,
That was his destination

The seas were rough
The waves were high,
Joseph muttered,
"Here I die"

The sea grew calm
The storm, it died
" Land is Ho"
The sailor cried

The men were tired, and some were ill
When they set foot upon the hill
The men were weary, "weary all"
They set up camp, before nightfall

Just before he went to bed,
Young Joseph, with his rod
He raised his staff above his head
And in the name of God,

He planted "holy" in the ground
And with a mighty shout,
"I claim this land for Christendom,
We'll drive those pagans out"!

Now, we come to modern times
The story to unravel
The pagans came from near and far
To "weary", more to travel

Then, up the road, in Worthy Farm
Another chapter bringing,
The Bands, they came from round the world,
And they started singing!

I've oft been to avalon,
I sought to find the answer,
The spirits, they keep telling me,
You're just another...
Chancer !

Author notes

A quirky little town in Somerset, uk. A town of
magic, legend, mystery (and ley lines). Also, A bit
of a Shindig, - just for fun, but once a year...

Hamish

See yon Hamish, there he goes
His Rods are perpendicular
What's he doing? No one knows
Well, nothing in particular
He's out again by early light
(He gave the horses such a fright!)
He had a talent, quite a gift
Master of the "Paradigm Shift"
What shift am I pertaining to?
What has been implied?
Let's regard yon Hamish,
Let him be your guide.
Way back in the mists of time,
Many were involved
From Pharaohs to the common man
The Dowsing art evolved.
You take a stick, or bob, or stone
Done in groups, or done alone,
Then you wait for it to twitch
You may even get an itch!
Tune yourself to "Cosmic Mind"
You never "ken" what you will find!
It's a gift we all once had,
But then we lost it,
Oh how sad.
Yon Hamish, as I said before,
His Rods were like a "Tiller"
He found he had the Dowsing "gift"
His name was,
Hamish Miller!!

c.Smudge 10/04/19

Cliches

I've bounced a ball
I've held a gun
Had some tears
Had some fun
I faced my fears
All bar one
What happens next?
I'm not sure
I think this madness has no cure

Author notes

After some time in exile, much reflection, alas, none the wiser

Melancholia ¿

So begins another day
Affirmations done
Will it be the perfect day?
Or just a humdrum one
Out the door I go
My fortune for to find
Walking through a puddle
There's something on my mind...
The pursuit of happiness
That's what we desire
But most of us alas, I think
End up in the mire!
Many years of counselling
To salve my shattered soul
Said the councillor, unto me,
" you have to have a goal "
Easier said than done, I say
And I've read all the books
More money for the author
That's the way it looks!
Perceive, believe, receive
Therein the secret lies
To get the things you want in life
You must visualise
Ten thousand affirmations
These you must recite
Half way through, I had a thought:
What a load of shite!

To make your dreams come true, is hard
Therein lies the rub
Am I to continue?
Or just go down the pub..

Author notes

Just a meandering, cynical view of the new age
movement

Empty Space

Just got up at 4am
Another day has started
Lost my bloomin keys now,
My patience has departed
I think I will go back to bed
I'm tired of all of this!
There's got to be another way
I badly need some bliss
So, I'm on the '25
Chock a block as ever
I'm studying the number plates
Elvis tells me,
It's now or never!
Mindfulness, I thought
I'll try a bit of that!
Two hours eating chocolate,
I did feel such a prat!
Now, let's not be too critical,
The teachings have their place
What we really need though,
Is just a bit of...

Space...

Author notes

Stuck in the mother of all traffic jams, 1 fag left,
busting for a wee I thought
Get me outta here @!

Choices

Woke up from a slumber
It was a lovely dream.
Then I came to realise,
Life's not what it seems

You have your Wytches,, your Warriors
And your Shining Knights
And then you have the idiots
Starting all the fights

The posturing politicians
Plotting all the wars
Then you have your Charlatans,
(You also have your Whores!)

And then out of all of this
What actually do you get?
I wish I knew the answer,
I haven't found it yet!

All the years of searching
All the years of toil,
It seems I don't know anything
It makes my blood to boil!

Many years of research
(And howling at the moon!)
I think I will go crazy
If I don't find out soon!

Recall that Soldier with the Spear?
I found out that was me,
That's a problem I don't need
I think you may agree!

So, back to the drawing board
It's back again I go
Will somebody help me please,
I really need to know?

We all have our problems
We all would like to know
We have our social media,
But how far does that go?

Let me make it clear,
We're all here for the ride
But, then when a loved one dies...
Who gets to decide?

The [sea of] confusion

We swirl around in this menagerie
We listen hard, but sometimes never hear
I'm right, you're wrong, l think that's very clear
No, wait, you're wrong, it's me they need to hear
It seems you missed the point, let me explain
You haven't got a clue, you've lost the game...

Author notes
Do we really listen or, in an effort to get our point
across do we actually miss the real point,
By default

Walking...

We all walk the path, do we not..?
The rigours of conformity
Roll the dice, pitch and toss, or not..
The uphill battle, won and lost
Another day, win or lose,
Whichever journey you may choose
Comfort zone, or breaking free
The choice remains your own

A little trick, perhaps, you'll see..
Are we not one, or otherwise...
Then, shall we take the mighty leap..?
Jump into the abyss, with faith.
Then, what will be will be....

Author notes
There comes a time when we must gather, the wise
ones, the storytellers, and find a better way..
This is our time...

Darkness...

...can only prevail
When there is no light..
L ight
I s
G iven
H ere
T onight...

Author notes
We can vanquish the dark..
We've been here before...

J'aime les oiseaux

Oh, how I crave the bohemian life
Away from the mindless cacophony
Wherever you go, there you are, not me
Blast the purveyors of all the fake news
I never felt more like singing the blues
I'll balance my chakras, tune my guitar
I'll sleep in till noon and bathe in the stream
I'll venture to be a philosopher
The likes of which yet, has never been seen
Pass me the hookah and hand me the hash
I'll often get wasted, because I can
I'll talk to the trees and give them a hug
I'll stand on a mountain, feeling quite smug
I'll tame the wild horses, that's what I'll do
I'll take up my quill and write as I will
Who am I kidding?, it's just a pipe dream
Back to the asylum, to scream, it seems...
...." time for your medication" the nurse said..
As they dragged me screaming, back into bed..

Author notes
What is madness, anyway?...

Silent...

Last night,
I had a dream...
Or, not a dream..
So it would seem..
I dreamed about..
Ice cream..
Or was it.
My scream..
This dream..
My dream..
My..
Silent...
Scream...

Author notes

Contest/voice being held back/Filpsider- w.c 31
Late one Saturday night, watching a documentary
about Eric Clapton, who featured in a band called
Cream...

the passing

More over there than over here
Where did they go, I ask
The greatest of the great, now gone
I wonder where they went
All so sudden, out of the blue
Another funeral...
We all pretend to be happy..
Well, I, for one, am not!
So many conversations lost
Am I selfish, I ask?
The great conundrum is revealed...
It was nought but a dream....

govinder

Went for a saunter, down Magdalene Street
The isle of Avalon, town of mystery and magic
To those who believe...
Capering towards me, all hobbit-like
Barefoot, carrying a staff
A very long staff, it was
We passed..
" l dig the t- shirt, thanks for the memory "
So, we stopped, a moment in time..
We chatted about ' whispering Bob '
And the ' whistle test '
To where do you head, says l
To the park, he said
I have a tai-chi class waiting
Join me, if you wish, 11 am, prompt
Cappuccino, was my fuel
Myriad thoughts propelled me back
There he was, flailing his stick
I joined, we moved to the dance of the tao
Separate from time, in the void, oneness
We sat, we talked..
Quantum mechanics to poetry
No subject was off-limits
We melded in the flow
Two amoebas joined, to form more..
I still hear his gentle whisper...
In the stillness, two souls- forever
My dear friend..
govinder...

One of everything

One breath to live
" step to take
" job to do
" love to lose
" song to sing
" bell to ring
" poem to write
" fight to fight
" glorious sunset to behold
" life to live...
before I'm old...

Empath

Walking in a resplendent coat
Magnificent, maelificent
I see, blinded
The corporeal conundrum, confounds
And confuses me
To walk, where others tread
To feel, to exist, evaporate
Walking alongside, yet apart
Now this, I feel exists
Tendrils, thoughts trafficking
Apart, together, separated
The eyes, conjoined, consciousness confused
Where do they come from? abused, bemused
The thoughts, I mean
This sanguine gift, this curse
To see as others see,
To feel as they do..
To absorb...

Somnambulism

To dream, but not to sleep is the problem
Deprivation demands due diligence
Standing at the edge, how did I get there?
Awake next morning, torn, bruised and tattered
Caffeine affords the antidote, for now..
Myriad tasks performed, to allay nap
Debilitating apprehension grips
Valerian, greedily ingested
Nocturnal perambulation remains
Lock all the doors, snuff out the lights, goodnight!

The roll of the dice

George and Lennie,
Shooting the breeze, by the pond
George had a dream, Lennie had a mouse
" One day " he said
" We'll have our own cabin, and bunnies "
George was smart, see,
Lennie, kinda dumb.
George looked after him
Kept getting himself into a whole mess of trouble
The girl..
It wasn't his fault
Didn't know his own strength
Had to leave..
Start anew
This time...

The girl came calling, flirting
Petted her, kinda hard
Broke her neck..

Lennie ran, back to the pond
The search was on...
George found him, muttering
Got out his gun
Thunderclap..
Lennie was gone
" Guess I did him a favour,
an act of kindness "

Based on the classic
Of mice and men, by
John Steinbeck
Poor Lennie was becoming a burden, George didn't
seem to have any other choice..
...an act of kindness?...

Go all the way

One amassing a great fortune
The other, however

Attaining nothing to speak of
So, let's break it all down

Which to admire, and which to loathe
It's just a matter of choice

One, a plutocrat, oligarch
The other, most humble

The sociopath, uncaring
The aid-worker, helping

Dark psychology, dark triad
Morals absent, cunning

A paramour, to ease the stress
Money laundering tricks...

Machiavellian capers
Only the bold succeed

Merely all about the numbers
Faustian agreements

" Oh yeah, life is sweet, I'm winning "
The law of the jungle

The last big deal, secret meeting
Two taps, back of the head

This chapter, my friend, is over
Tag on the toe, John Doe

So, which would you prefer?

in vino veritas (or, many a slip..)

there was a man who had a plan,
he came from way down south
and, if I ever see that man
I'll punch him in the mouth!
the man was me, from years ago
I hardly recognise
the man has changed beyond belief
I can't believe my eyes!
the plan took time to formulate,
it took him many years
the plan, it sounded awesome,
after several beers!
the plan, it never came to pass
there's no way that it could
he tried the plan,
it didn't work
and it never would!

smoke and mirrors

confusion!
where are they?
where am I?
in this cloudy maelstrom
as if sinking in quicksand
(somebody give me a hand)
sinking fast, suffocating, choking
vision fading, the eternal miasma
ah! bliss, the devils kiss
the cold embrace of death!
neurons firing! dendrites pulsing!
so, this is what it's like
(mamma shoulda told me!)
I await my destiny...
the road less travelled...
not today my dear!...

marking time

I live the way i wish to live
that is my choice
by and by
I wore the tunic
I held the gun
battles lost and battles won
lovers won and lost, just for fun
I marched in time
I held my post
(I may have even seen a ghost!)
time marched on
and I marched with it
This only life,
I try to live it!
I fought alongside angels
we held the demons
but, to what cost?
life is bitter, life is sweet
the ones you lost,
the ones you meet
too many cliches
the poets say,
not enough "strong" words!
have I learned nothing?
I'll say it as it is!
Was this all for nought?
The simple fact remains
Given the choice...
by god! I'd do it all again!

Scarlet Woman (Scarlet Chronicles- act 1)

Young Mollie was a pretty lass
Loved by all who knew her
Little dimples on her cheeks
Her heart was kind and pure
Her uncle sat her on his lap
I'd like to marry you
Young Mollie didn't understand,
The girl was only two
Then it started happening
Each and every night
Her uncle crept into her room
He gave her such a fright

Mollie had to go to school
She studied really hard
The boys, they played their silly games
With Mollie, in the yard

Those days are now behind her
She put the ghosts to bed
But, sometimes every now and then
They pop into her head

Harry was a gentleman
A man of perfect stature
Lovely Mollie caught his eye

So, he set out to catch her
She agreed to meet him
Things turning out quite well
Maybe, they'll get married
Only time will tell...

Tonight's the night, our Mollie thought
I'll take him to the park
We'll go out for a lovely stroll
And do it after dark
Kissing, touching, probing
They writhed upon his coat,
Just before he climaxed,

She slit the bastards throat...

Author notes

An exploration into the cruel things people do, and
their consequences

Round and round (Scarlet Chronicles- act 2)

So there's the little strumpet
She thinks I cannot see her
Harlot incarnate
Brazen as you like
Murderess, I'll be bound
If you only knew
The man, he loved her dearly
That was clear to see
She sent him on his way
Crackled like a banshee,
Nothing more to say
Been watching her, I have
Message from the Met
Watch this one, she's dangerous
Closing in the net
I've met all sorts
Killers, pimps and chancers
I have my means....
Even a couple of pole dancers
They weren't bad, just misguided
Good informants they were
And good for the ride
Everyone happy....
Back to the bedsit, I suppose
Watch the Millwall lose again
Bit of Scotch, then bed

Strange one this, public school,
Ponys, the lot
Where did it all go wrong?
Another incident, got the brief
Business man, throat slit
Wife and kids
Whitechapel, business as usual
That sucks, doesn't it?
Met her once, glassed a bloke in a pub
Now, here's the rub,
Butter wouldn't melt
Heard it all before
Who makes these people?
Damned if I know
Another shout, gotta go
Everyone happy...

Author notes

Poor Mollie, I'll be bound

C'est la vie

The times were hard
I've been to hell
I once heard a tolling bell
I walked away, with me intact!
(I nearly even made a pact)
The Faustian tale, I know it well
I'm not going back to hell
I'm happy here
With all its woes
The wounding slings, and arrows
The gift of life, is so sublime
We hardly notice passing time
But in the end, back to source
The hare and tortoise run their course
It's up to us, how we prevail
Will we win, or will we fail?
It's all about the state of mind
What we lose, or what we find
You have to pace yourself, you see
What is winning? You tell me
Life's big questions, what will be?
That being said....
C'est la vie

mater

Mother didn't like me
She told me once or twice
That really hurt my feelings
It wasn't very nice
The years rolled on
As they will
Poor mother now is dead
Left a mighty chasm
So many things unsaid
I joined a band of brothers
So many battles won
One day I got a medal
For something that I done
Would mother like me now?
After all this time?
I just can't think of any way
To finish off this rhyme

41

Mabel

So ere' I am again
Attackin' all the weeds
Them bloomin' crows an' magpies
'Ave ate up all me seeds!
An' bloomin' nex' doors cat
'E mus be out at dawn
The bugger left a partin' shot
An' crapped upon me lawn!
I love me rhododendrons
They are me pride an' joy
I like to sit outside each day
Me labours to enjoy!

Barometer says fine
I 'ope their aint a frost
Ol' jack, 'e caught me out las' year
Me plants an' flowers lost!
I miss me poor ol' Mabel
She can't be 'ere ter see
I'm goin' back inside now,
To ave a cuppa tea

selfie !?

Oh, thou wicked selfie
Parading all your vanity!
With your ma, or with a star
Surrendering your sanity

Part Two: Starstruck

The Cosmic Joke

Just practicin' me art
The craft of sages
Much venerated
Thro' the ages

I wish to tell a tale, or two
Will anybody listen
Well, will you?

I tell tales of luck and valour
Some stories dark,
Of clammy pallor

One tale in particular springs
To mind
The ageless story of mankind

The Nothingness did have a dream
"I wish to laugh, I wish to scream
I need some fellowship,
So it would seem,
More than just to dream and dream"

So the Nothingness set about
Her womb was filled
With fear and doubt
She gave a heave and pushed it out!

Out into the empty void
Her spawn, it travelled, an Asteroid
The Unmanifest, some would say
A substance made,
And it was clay!

For six light days
The Implings played
Then balls of light
Were all arrayed

For Billlenia , peace was found
Harmony, tranquillity all around

Then one night and it was black
The Cosmos heard a mighty crack!
The Cauldron split, cast asunder
Then there was the loudest thunder

The next Billenia was uncertain
There descended the darkest curtain
The pealing of a cosmic bell
The whole "shebang" was sent to Hell!

Then at noon, the battle started
It seemed the Gods had all departed
Good and Evil, Yin and Yang
Then there was an awful bang

And then nothing, nothing more
Save one survivor, the Cosmic Whore...

She laid her head and, it would seem,
The Nothingness did have a dream...

Scoundrel

There he is, the little knave
Causing mischief, no one's safe!
From the cradle to the grave,
His road to hell, he will pave

One lovely sunny day,
Only took a couple hours
More mischief on the way,
He took out both the Towers

Back in the beginin'
He sought to start them sinnin'
An Apple and a Snake
And he just stood there grinnin'

Then one day, he made a spear
This will do the trick!
I'll fill them full of fear,
Then she'll get out quick!

No rest for the wikkid
That's the way it seems,
One day he'll come and join you
He'll get into your dreams!

He knows what you want,
He knows what you fear,
He knows how to control you,
He does it ev'ry year!

"So, is there any hope?"
I hear some of you say
It may sound like a joke,
But pray my friend, just pray

So what's he up to now?
Let's take a little look,
Cancer, Aids, Ebola
A Billion souls he's took !

It doesn't look too good,
I think we all agree
There is another way
Just harken unto me

You must listen to your Soul
And you will be set free!

Back unto the Scoundrel
Beneath the big spotlight
His Mother should have told him,
"Son, you'll be alright"

grey

Out of the primordial sludge
He rose, his name was Smudge
Him birthed from the Cosmic Whore
The Cosmos would never be the same
No more
He was made of clay,
That's why he looks so grey!
he traversed eternity
To try and save his sanity
And it was bloody cold
to add to his misery!
So the bitch abandoned me,
Am I lost? we shall see
Sounds like the Scoundrel
I hear you say
Yeah, I met him, not impressed
I sent him far away!
Sent him to a Godforsaken place
Light years away,
the other end of space!
He was my brother, don't you see,
Doesn't look a bit like me!
The wise amongst you may agree
Bit of sibling rivalry!!
On again, it may sound tragic
It was me, inventing magic
Magic with a C, you see

We need no K,
You may agree
Anyway, I do digress
I have a maiden to undress!
She fancies me, I must confess,
What happened next, I'll let you guess!

So, back to the scoundrels' brother
(The one deserted by his mother)
She was me and I was she-
I loved her like no other
Then I heard the Cauldron split
I thought, my God we're in the shit!
This all happened once before,
The perpetrator? Cosmic Whore!

Then it happened once again
The Cosmic dust, the acid rain
Shall we make the same mistake?
We have to change, for all our sakes
Back again to recent times
The Grey Magician, With his rhymes
Magic with a C not K
I'll change the world without delay!
I can make you well
Or I can make you sick
I can do it all
With just a finger click!

The final choice is yours
We've all been here before
Do we make the quantum leap?

(Embracing Natural Law)
Or all go round and round again
To wake the Cosmic Whore ?...

We are the "gods"

We possess many things
we own nothing!
We are children of the stars
but, we don't know
somebody asked me about theDao
I said, "I don't know"
(only meant as a guide)
we have been strangled,
suffocated
but, still the yearn to learn
Pandora's Box?
The opening
what shall we find?
The Ark of the Covenant
Illumination or, radiation ?
Break through the confusion,
shatter the illusion!
Come on, my brethren
we're better than this
have we not had
the Angel's kiss?
just a bit discombobulated
we are so near, yet so far
the endless jostling
the self-important posturing
we sit in our bedsit
railing at the moon!

WhatsApp , twitter, whatever
shall we start again?
Or, is it too late?
But wait,
if the gods (?) don't have us
then, they have nothing!
(no dice to play)
we hold sway!
This is our day
embrace the sunrise
just remember
they cast us down!

—   because they couldn't do it
WE ARE THE GODS
If only we knew it!...

Author notes
We are lightbeings – believe!

Bang!

We are not of this Earth
Check your DNA!
We came from the stars
We came from afar
Pleiades springs to mind...
The missing link
The cosmos blinked
Genesis of homo sapiens
What did we bring to the table?
I'd rather not say...
I am not able
We made a mistake
The heavens quacked
Original sin?
Just look within
Have we gone too far?
Was it all for naught
Perhaps, we should be asking Gort
Klaatu Barada Nikto
Just look around at what you see
The Cosmos unfolds ceaselessly
Just look about
Beauty and wonder
All we did, was pillage and plunder
In the grandest scheme of things
We don't matter, Gabriel sings
So, what went wrong?

It's hard to say
The blueprint failed
We've had our day..
The architects, they got it wrong
The Angels knew it all along
What else is there left to say,,
Armageddon on its way

Author notes
Another stab at the meaning of it all.....

Leo

I reside in the fifth
Bask in the sun
Forged in the fire
The Leonine one

Part Three: Myth, Magick (and darker things...)

The realm of fae

I once met a faerie and oh, she was wee
That day beneath the Lilac tree
I once met a faerie and oh she could dance
I was so beguiled l, lost in a trance
The lady from fae, we sat for a while
She told me some stories
She so made me smile
She told me of Elfame, and unicorn Kings
She gave me a warning, about darker things
If l were a faerie, I'd never get old
I'd dwell like a Prince, in a castle of gold
She taught me the ' craft '
The ways of the Fae
We once knew the Faeries
But pushed them away
You may hear a tinkle, a chuckle, a song...
And think you imagine, but then
You'd be wrong ...
We laughed, we sang, we danced, we tarried
She made me a faerie, and now, we are
Married

Quality Time

cave quid volunt :
Be careful what you wish for..

My mausoleum, eight by ten
I languish in the holding pen

Pestilence, outside the door
I cannot venture out, no more

Conversations on the Web
My sanity, it starts to ebb...

Zoom meeting with the client
Locked away, so compliant

Halcyon days- distant past
How long will this sentence last..

I turn to substance, ease the pain
The liquor, simply rots the brain

Hallucinations challenge me
No quite believing what l see

Music practice, poetry..
No stimulation- none for me..

But then again- a game to play..
The **grimoire** that l hid away

Incantation- circle cast
Did the study- had the fast

Vision now, out of focus
what a bunch of hocus- pocus

The air is chilled- the rising stench
The pact is made- l feel the wrench

Surrounded now, filled with fear
The dark, decaying atmosphere..

This apparition torments me...
But now, at least....
.... some company.....

Opening the gate

abyssus abyssum invocat:
One false step leads to another:
Literal translation: he calls Hell

Mr Scaramouche an upright and studious man
Learned, and most meek..
Honourable.
Vocabulary, and intellect, profound
Seeker of the truth
And other most alarming concepts
The day, most memorable,
When they first met..
Disturbed and perturbed him,
Most penetratingly...
...took to his bed..
Succumbed to an acute case of..
...the ' vapours '
For one whole season, and one half
Palpitations, hallucinations,
The poor man, perplex't
...was given to visions..
Of the most inconvenient kind
He spoke in tongue, and rhyme..
The Emerald book, was on his mind
The curs'd tablet, he could not find

One such chapter, to recall
Infernal episode, to best them all
Beelzebub, the Lord of it
Scaramouche, beckon'd to the pit
" Belay your tact, say I"
" I have a meeting, I must fly "
Unfinished business, pulled him back
Oblivion engulfing...
..black as black...

[shapeshifter]

My mask, cunningly contrived
Deliciously, deliriously derived

I walk amongst the many,
Chosen by the few...

Metamorphosis enacted
Creating something new...

Shape-shifting, a changeling born
This miasmic tapestry..
The faces I have worn

The brief, ephemeral creature
The time, it seems to fly

Cocooned within the chrysalis
So now...
It's here...
I lie...

Keeping her keys

a subtle invitation

Do you wish to commune, my Queen?
The key offered, most unusually proffered
The witchfire calls, pulling, compelling
The torch, within my hands..
Illicits the insatiable hunger
For truth
Primal forces to urge...
Opening the temple within
The light, casting shadows..illuminating..
The sovereign Witch..
A cruel mistress, to regard
Having her needs..
To follow, is to be all consumed, purged
Reminded of the ancient divinity
Once cherished, beloved, banished then
The torch, ever brighter burning
To be chosen before time..
Finally accepting, embracing

     ...my Queen...

Author notes
A brief journey into the world of Witchcraft, or
indeed, their Queen..Hekate...

Pronounced eh- kah- teh. The first...Queen of the witches, guardian of the crossroads and indeed, keeper of the keys. An unforgiving mistress, only in as much as she encourages her devotees to make tough decisions. To look at their situation through the eyes of truth. Thus, freeing themselves from the shackles of delusion, embracing their authentic self, as it should be...

Magus

from the red book...

The Sapphire twilight descending
Turgid torpor tempted

I would cast my hand, to summon....

sacred geometry...

Written with diligence, and fear
Circle, now completed

Encapsulated, in the flame
The atmosphere, is chilled

The ancient call, the borneless ones
To be stirr'd, awoken

The vowels carefully vibrate
Aligned with Cosmic hum...

As it was, Angelic message
Past revealed, to the few

The sign of Osiris, enter'd
My blade, to pierce the star

The seventy-two legions rise
.... demonic chattering....

Sulphurous halitosis burns..
Brimstone, permeating

The Cosmic correspondences
Copiously copied

" As to why have we been summoned "
...for, to open...
            ... the gate..

Body snatchers

Could there ever have been such a heinous pair?
William Burke and William Hare
Back in 1828
Met by chance, cast by fate
Robert Knox, he tipped the wink
Offered money, made them think
A new diabolical profession
To satisfy a dark obsession
Cadavers gathered, all exhumed
' Auld Reekie's' back, it was assumed
The Constable's, they rallied round
But, Burke and Hare, just went to ground
A snitch, the pair were apprehended
Their life of crime was promptly ended
Habeas Corpus- day in court
The Judge presiding, had a thought
I'll toss a coin, if you agree
And, if you win, I'll set you free..
Voices in the courtroom rang...
The penny fell...
The pair did hang..

Agenda

New World Order- the great re-set?
Conspiracy, or fact...
Occidental shift of power
Born in the lab, could that be true?
Global lockdown ensues
" We have the science, stay at home-
Want to meet, then use the phone "
The masses gather, had enough
Batons raise, cops get tough
Is there any way out of this?
" Get your jab"- Satan's kiss
A 'deadly' new strain emerges
World leaders have their say...
You can't take away our freedom..
Final two words...no way!

Dreamscape

Descending into peaceful slumber
R.E.M the journey begins
Ethereal images morph
Astral journeys undertaken
Miasmic metaphors mesmerise
Sublime suggestions secreted
Corpus Callosum connections collide
Angelic choirs to lift the soul
Pituitary gland awakens third eye
Enlightenment...soon forgotten...

The ancient call

Eco eco Adonnai, eco eco Malkuth
The lesser banishing ritual preformed
Sign of the enterer
The pentagram burning blue
The goetia is summoned
To feed the Egregore
The watchers in attendance
Nephilim cast down
Will rise again, by Mages hand
Truth confounded by tricksters tongue
Black mirror shattered
Evil devices, the portal entices
Cosmic consciousness corrupted
Sapiens progress interrupted

Slither...

On hallows eve, the veil is thin
The creatures gather from within
In dark, malevolent splendour
One such creature, sent from hell
It lurks inside the wishing well
I've only seen it once before
I heard it scratching at my door
I went to see who beckons me
But, nothing there for me to see..
A dark, foreboding fantasy
I went outside, to get some air
Surely, there was something there..
Just beside the lilac tree
A dark phantasm looked at me
My sanity was fading
The tendrils, all pervading
It feeds, it needs another soul...
And many more, to make it whole
My friend, this tale is true..
And now....
We come...
For you.....

Alchemy

Where is the Philosopher's Stone?
Does it even exist?
The Alchemists sought this jewel
Long ago, it was prized
Trismegistus had always known
Thrice great, it has been said
The Emerald Tablet alludes..
Base metal, into gold
Many have tried, only to fail
Or, is there another?
The primordial slime of man
To become...
The Divine..

Author notes

The legend, is it about metal, or mettle?

Eve

in a garden
long ago
little girl
she wished to know
bit an apple
from a tree
cursed mankind
apparently....

Pithos [The Urn]

The stars incline, they don't compel
The coming fate, the final bell
The denizens of Hades
Awakening to feed
The gods around the cauldron
Produce the demon seed
Eve was not the first, you see
The first was made of clay
The gift of fire was stolen
The Pithos sent to Earth
Prometheus was banished
The human race was cursed
The urn was full of secrets
The mysteries of life
She went to Epimetheus
Who took her for his wife
The Pithos held a caveat
For knowledge, you must pay
She clutched the urn against her chest
And quickly stole away..
Remembering the warning
Temptation was too strong
Removed the stopper from the urn
Then, realised she was wrong
The demons spiralled upwards
The hate, the pain, the greed
Pandora, by the will of Zeus
Released the demon seed...

Spear

The little man, he's standin'
There gazin' at the cross
The man upon the cross looked down,
He feels a sense of loss

"My lord, I do implore you
What am I to do "
"My son, no greater deed to do,
You have to run me through!"

" My lord, I am afraid, say I
This deed, you ask me for...
I feel, within my heart of hearts,
I'm breakin' natural law!

" My son, my son, hear me now
There is no other way..
This deed for me, you have to do,
You have to save the day..

The soldier, he did tremble,
And then, with all his might
He plunged his Spear deeply in,
And promptly died of fright!!

The Spear, however, on that day
The spear, it did not die
The spear, it merely slippt' away
T' had other fish to fry!!

Whomever owns the Spear they say,
One thousand years to rule
The spear descended quietly,
Within the house of Thule

A wily little Austrian
With lustin' for success,
He hid the spear within his coat,
The nation, to address

" If you will but follow,
This I do decree
We'll clear the world of all the scum,
And I will set you free.":

He gave them all a little song..
And this they sang with 'glee '
From all the bars and halls and squares..
'Tomorrow belongs to me '!

Back again, unto the spear,
It was a wily thing..
The spear had other plans, you see
And other songs to sing...

Al Hazred

I found a little book inside a church
It hid behind a brick upon the wall
Just went inside, to shelter from the rain
I knew my life would never be the same
I held the tome within my hands and wept
In thirty years, I've hardly even slept
The elder ones, they beckoned me, that day
The hounds of hell, are never far away
The Arcane wisdom here, within my hands
I'm bending space and time, to suit my will
The trickster Marduk, he is on his way
Was banished there, forever and a day
The battle raged, and tore the skies apart
Oblivion, extinction, came to pass
The book, you see, it prophesied the end
They're coming back, to do it all again...

Author notes

Al Hazred, the "mad monk" brought to life by H.P
Lovecraft, reputedly found the most diabolical,
dangerous book, ever written.

the hellbound bar

Had to take a little walk
just around the block
the girlfriend see, she stole his cash
and his beloved Hi Rok

young Jude, he's not a drinking man
it's not about the booze
thought he'd have a beer
(what's he got to lose?)

he found his own oasis
there before his eyes
the bar, last week it wasn't there
What a fine surprise

half price bud, free wi-fi
come on in,
don't be shy

the barmaid (slightly skeletal)
"I'll fix a drink for you,
I'll make for you a cocktail
it's called-
The Devil's Brew"

the jukebox, it was blaring
it was a song he knew
that old Jay Hawkins classic
"I' put a spell on you!"

sipping at his cocktail
and feeling rather fine
an eerie feeling gripped him
(it was a warning sign)

as he turned to walk away
the barmaid gripped his arm
he felt the icy clutch of death
(the bar had lost its charm!)

the place, it took a different hue
and rising from the floor
screeching, grotesque creatures
just more and more and more

surrounded now,
there's no way out
he tried to scream,
but nought came out

they had him in their clutches
he heard the closing bell
your time is up, you're leaving now
to stay with us in
HELL

Pandora!

Pained, anxious, troubled
Angst, rising like bile
Now, she has a plan!
Determined to make a difference
Only one problem
Remember what they said?...
Axis shift, no stopping it now...

Author notes
Another acrostic, I know! Can't help it, they just come...
Save me ??

assassin

A bland, unassuming individual
Seriously inconspicuous
So thorough and meticulous
Amazing knowledge in the art of killing
Stealthy, and slightly chilling
Sangfroid, sanguinary, sardonic
Imbued with talent so demonic
Novichok, perfume, how ironic!

Author notes
An exercise in acrostic

owetoenn

Only one life?
I beg to differ
Various times, I've visited
Judged for many felonies!
Kharmik rules apply
Patiently, I wait my turn
Just to play the game
Hoping this time
Given grace
Victory will be mine!
Denizens, they wait for me
Encapsulate my soul
Undercurrents of the past
Gather round like jackals
Xenophobia, I've been there!
Alluding to supremacy
But I will, to travel on
Much to learn
So little time
Task at hand
Horizons new, as I explained
Win or lose
Nothing ventured, nothing gained!

Author notes
Being tasked to pen an Acrostic, using a list of
random letters, ergo O to N !!!

song of vice and ire

big ned lost his head
joffrey lost his voice
went to dine and took some wine
he really had no choice!
jon snow, full of woe
his final watch
he'll have to go
red wedding, no bells there,
just blood and mayhem everywhere
took a ride on a dragon
the little guy liked his flagon
moon door, don't go there
or you'll be flying through the air
ramsey got bit, and that was it!
(bastard? just a bit)
the final battle for the throne
danny done for,
should've known
aria killed the icy king
(ed sheeran even got to sing!)
nearly done, final word
seven kingdoms ruled by a bird?
hail the bard! (and hbo)
now i really have to go

Author notes
Just a playful summary of an epic show, some may
like it, I don't know

The enchantress

Hypnotic rhythm, paradise given
Willowing, billowing, flowing, glowing
The tantalising mystery
Beguiling men thro' history
A body built for sin!
Let the dance begin...

Throne

Young Cersei did the walk of shame
On Sparrows high decree,
She walked, parading all her wares
For all the world to see
First, they cut her hair off,
Then, they stripped her bare.
Shame, shame, shame they cried!
(She had a lovely pair!)
Down and down the steps, she went
And so the insults came.
Revenge was surely on her mind
("I'll set them all aflame")
But, still her power grew and grew.
"I'll take the Iron Throne,
If Jamie will not help me
I'll do it on my own!"
Oh. Cersei's mind was wicked,
As wicked as it gets
"I'm a Lannister, you see, we always pay our debts!"

Author notes
Penned on a balcony in Dubrovnik, drinking rum,
after visiting ' the steps of shame' June 2019

Standing

Standing by the gates of Hell
I hear the tolling of the bell
The name they called,
It was not mine
Maybe I'll die another time

Salteador de caminos

[The Highwayman]

He watches, waits and listens
His prey will be here soon
He waits a while longer,
Beneath the frosty moon

Hark, I hear them coming
The hooves upon the earth,
I will give them such a fright,
I'll find out what they're worth

"Stand and deliver"
This command he gave
The driver shot him in the eye
And sent him to his grave!

There is a moral to this tale
And it may make you titter,
You'll find out what the moral is,
On instagram or twitter!

Part Four: A call to arms

The Regiment

Way back in the desert war
The Panzers were advancing
Meanwhile, back in " Blighty Town "
The gentry, they were dancing
Montgomery, with a steely glare
He held a somber meeting
" That upstart, Rommel, I declare
He surely needs defeating "
They said as one-
" It can't be done "
The war machine, kept whirling
Then, out of nowhere, like a ghost
He came, his name was Stirling
" I have a plan " the Major said
" Forgive me all my sins "
I also have a motto, and that is
"WHO DARES WINS "
The top brass, they were gathered
They cried, " you surely jest!"
The Major cried
" you'll eat your words,
My lot will be the best!"
The Major went and found them,
And what a motley bunch
The Adjutant had news to bring,
Disturbing Churchill's lunch!
The minister, he listened-

His patience, not enduring,
I have, you see, he said, with glee
A man, named Alan Turing
" But sir, " the Adjutant replied
"I'll get you up to speed
The desert war, is all but lost,
It's these men, that we need "
" young man, young man, hear what I say
Still, I cannot see it
If this project were to fail then
On your head would be it!"
It came to pass,
The deeds were done
The "glory boys "
The battle won
Just one final thought,
It may be hard to swallow
If you have them by the balls
Their "HEARTS AND MINDS " Will follow!!

Author notes

Conceived by a chance meeting in the pub, with a
stranger
Something that he said,
Reminded me of the
Halcyon days, when we thought we could fly, hell,
some of us even had
H.A.L.O s

16 Princess Gate (South Kensington)

The shots rang out, that was the sign
The terrorists had crossed the line
Now before the whole world's eyes
The fearsome group would mobilize.

Red team abseiled down, Blue team set the charges
The Nimrod Plan was underway
The tension there, enlarges.

The curtains twitch, there was a hitch,
The drapes, they caught alight.
The man called Oan was on the phone,
He got shot on sight!

There was a crash, a thunderflash,
Got thrown into the mix.
The terrorists did realise,
That they were in a fix.

The hostages were gathered,
And all put to one side.
Then Nijad saw his chance
He went with them to hide.

Young MacAleese, he saw it,
He spotted all of this
He pulled young Nijad to his feet
And dealt a "Glasgow Kiss"

11 minutes later, that's all the time it took,
Maggie Thatcher's author, he put it in his book!

When the dust had settled,
The lads got sent to court
The Barrister, he told them,
"I'll give you food for thought"

Then the orders came, they came from high
command
The lads went back to Hereford
With just a reprimand!

The one that didn't

Get away..
Back at the "lines"
A call to muster
That's it- bluff and bluster
Early morning briefing
The "pledge" we are "badged"
We are the "chosen ones"
Jesus, this is it!
Now, we're heading for the shit!
Been on a few tours
But, now this is war!
Put on some Dire Straits
"Brothers in arms"
That'll do the trick 1
(I just bloody feel sick!)
Mobilise!
The H.A.L.O drop
Mind focused now,
I'm invincible!
The desert ain't just sand
You had to be there
Just remember the motto,
And you'll be fine
Gashed me leg!
Don't hurt a bit
On autopilot now
Took out a few planes

Causing bloody mayhem!
Then, it all went wrong
Don't know why
(Maybe write a book one day!)
The machinations of torture
Think of a spot, then focus
Nothing prepares you
You are dead!
The grey fog of denial and pain
Diplomacy (and backhanders) rules the day!
We got sent home
Sobering thoughts
I hit the booze
And turned to Buddha
And then, the nightmares!
You're never the same!
I prayed to God
-He didn't answer
We live to fight another day
(maybe live a different way)...

Author notes

the "poem" I shouldn't have wrote ! this is for my old
pals, half of them are dead now, had to get it off my
chest..

Ten past eight

follow- on from ' The one that didn't'...

The mission, ill conceived, at best
A complete clusterfuck

We were mobilised, the first time
Find the ' Scuds', and destroy

Hastily prepared plans were passed
Needless to say, captured!

Stripped naked, stress- position
The beatings, regular..

The ' hoodings' and ' waterbording'
- Yes, they did it as well..

Oh, but there was much worse to come..
Psychological ' tricks '

" I bring you news, your Mother died"
The false ' executions '

The baying crowds outside, bloodlust
All hungry for revenge

One fine morning, all hell broke loose..

The lads came to get us

Back to the ' Lines' for a de-brief
..The time was..
..... ten past eight...

Author notes
Army poster]
Travel the World
Meet interesting people..
and shoot them..
...a cynical recollection

O'er the hills

Ho, ye lads, here's forty shillin's
Stand on me, hoist the flag
Ride with Wellin'ton, by his side
Purge the userpers, aye

I'll sing ye a song, play the fife
Marchin' off to glory
Sun's up, muster all ye can
Lost another thousand

Georgie boy, thank's ye kindly, aye
Wellin'ton for glory
Stand- to boys, three rounds a minute
Lost another thousand

Corsican lad, he's on the run
Take up the fife and drum
Georgie boy, would like to meet ye
After he's stuffed his whore

Author notes

Based on the song ' over the hills and far away,' by
John Tamms, pertaining to the Napoleonic wars,
featured in the award winning TV series
Sharpes Rifles, starring the most excellent actor
Sean Bean....

Part Five: Limerick

Revenant

There was a Pallbearer named smudge
Throughout life, he harboured a grudge
He stood by the grave
His soul, for to save
His colleagues, then gave him a nudge

Author notes

The author, being challenged by a colleague to pen a poem regarding Pallbearing, ergo...

Pertaining to the word' nudge '
Is the nudge for good, or evil?
The paradox emerges...

Portal

a dark limerick chain ?

The view is so stunning, my dear
The air is remarkably clear
So, what should you do?
We're waiting for you
Step in, you have nothing to fear

Pact
I'm glad you decided to come
The journey, most deadly, for some..
Remember your Pact
A matter of fact
To my will, you must now succumb

Premise
You made an unbreakable deal
A most foolish action, I feel
You asked to be free
A folly, you see..
So, now then, before me, you kneel

Perdition
Your judgement, is soon to be passed
The dice, unmistakably cast
On having the facts
Your most heinous acts
Have surely engulfed you...
...at last...

Author notes

Based on the classic tale of Faust, and his
somewhat questionable deal with the Devil..

Glimmer

I saw a sight that was most rare
To see a man, who wasn't there
Pulsating spectre
Some ghostly vector
That vision, gave me quite a scare

Author notes
Loosely based on the poem
' yesterday, upon the stair, l saw a man, who wasn't
there
Author unknown

Languid

(a simple limerick chain ?)

Late
I always end up being Late
It seems, just a product of fate
My clock is awry
I watch the time fly
The deadlines will just have to wait..

Languish
It seems I must clean up my act
A most irrefutable fact!
When put to the test
I'm way past my best
The last job I had, I got sacked!

Lassitude
I'm busy just dossing around
No ' get-up- and-go' to be found
There's so much to do
I don't have a clue
My vigour has fell to the ground

Saviour faire

I find it extremely distasteful
It's also enormously wasteful
To open a book
And not even look
This conduct, I feel is disgraceful

Author notes

Carpe hunk libre

Angling and dangling..

I went off to fish by the stream
Was planning on catching some Bream
But, when it got dark
Got bit by a Shark
Thank God it was only a dream..

Baggins

The halfling, he came from the shires
Adventure, is what he desires
He found a ring
He heard it sing
Now it's off to Grey Lakes, it transpires

Author notes

Big story, little poem...

shopping

There was a young lady called Fay
Who went into town for the day
She baought some nice shoes
And drank some nice booze
And when she got home
She said, yay !

Author notes

Inspired by my friends favourite comment YAY!

untitled

there was a young man from kinross
who never remembered to floss
one night with a shout
"my teeth have fell out"
each day he'd lament at his loss

Author notes

Another journey into the strange, quirky world of
the limerick (upon study, none of the limerick that
I read have titles- hence...) enjoy

ode to Bettie

There was a young lady named Bettie
born by the end of the jetty
she met a guy
who made her cry
how sad- some guys-so petty

Author notes

just meandering into the world of the limerick, there
is one whom I know, allowed me to show so, here
goes, I'm now in the thick of it!

Writers Block

Intended to write a Pentameter
The problem, I'm only an amateur
Got the iambic wrong
The lines were too long
I just couldn't grasp the parameter

Part Six: [haiku]

[haiku]

matsuo bashō
gazed upon the lotus
and all was revealed

[lightning]

blinding light of life
transgressing back to the source
...and so it goes on...

[parables]

if this is so good
why do we quest for more
what is the answer..

[hawk]

she rises in flight
aeronautical splendour
questioning it all...

[twilight]

blackbird rejoices
sun gives way to Sapphire sky
stars greet rising moon

[slumber]

the dawn breaks
sun rises
snooze button

[dandy lions]

dandelions bloom
fluttering fairylike fall
gardeners delight!

[buddha]

sticky hand rises
buddha learned final lesson
ascended master

[judgement]

nebiru returns
ancient gods to re- emerge
yet, what have we learned

[wu wei]

effortless action
water- gentle- calm- yet strong
trying not to try

Author notes

The tao- the way never acts, but nothing is left
undone

[mudra]

unlocking the gift
chakras gently opening
kundalini rise

[clouds]

pareidolia
to see faces in objects
your face forever

[inspiration]

meandering thoughts
trickle into consciousness
inspiration flows

[asana]

sun salutation
the path of least resistance
master of my fate

[visitors]

the annunaki
travelled from the twelfth planet
marduk has arrived...

[rainbow]

Celestial orb
Prismatic colours explode
On heaven's canvas

[familiar]

Metamorphosis
She helps me with my magic
Not just a feline

Author notes

The witches familiar, shape shifter, can manipulate
reality

[tears]

The weeping reptile
Falsification of grief
Not to be trusted

..

[loch]

the lake they call ness
aquatic leviathan ~
surfacing to feed

Author notes

Based on the legend of the Loch Ness monster,
bonnie Scotland, true story? 'course it is...

Living (haiku)

The weekend is here
To play, to sing, to enjoy
To free the spirit

Author notes

Happy weekend

[blackbird]

Black velvet plumage
sweet articulate refrain
brings joy to us all

Author notes

Just sending a tweet to ya'll

[rejoice]

behold all is well
it's not just any old day
so much more than that

Author notes
Haiku, just haiku

[matin]

the sun hued glimmer
the cacophony begins
all is wonderful

Author notes

my second (feeble) dabblings with haiku. oh well,
may as well put it out there, blinking in the light of
the morning sun. it's a beautiful world, if viewed
through the correct lens

Part Seven: Cinquain

666

Crowley
The Magician
Thelema Theurgy
He summoned the demons from hell
The beast...

Okupayemost

Salisbury
Quaint little town
Red spectre on its way
Novichok wrapped up in a bow
Payback

Author notes

Dastardly dealings dealt deftly

Experiment

Stanford
Inmates and screws
All going well, for now
Brutality, rapings, beatings
Cancelled

Author notes

Stanford prison experiment.
14-21st August 1971. When you peel away the
psyche, there will be consequences, always.
The [id] is never far away..

Statistics

Sickness
Emergency
Loved ones gathered, praying
Ventilator scorching, burning
Flatline------

Author notes

The apocalypse, or the agenda ?

Covid

Test tube
Exponential
World wide pandemic now
The beast is released from the lab
Job done

Author notes

Is what it is. Thanks to the Bush poet for teaching
me this style, hope she's happy, wherever she is
(she'll be right)

H.A.L.O

Green light
Ready to fly
Done my checks good to go
Descending through cumulous veils
Deployed!

Author notes

What kind of man...? A feeble attempt at describing an High Altitude Low Opening parachute drop, through the eyes of cinquain

lucifer

cast down
fallen angel
I will bring you wisdom
If you will but follow always
you're mine

Author notes
just for the"hell" of it!

Guilt

Did it
No going back
Blood on my hands for sure
Time to ponder dastardly deeds
Sorry

Author notes

My first attempt at cinquain, probably the last!
Why do I do this to myself!!

Afterword:

[so now it is done...]

The writers craft (C-Raft)...
Craft n. Occupation requiring skill...
Craft: boat, ship, aircraft or spaceship!
So, if you break it down, removing the C. (or sea),
you get raft: floating platform of logs!
That would be a fitting analogy! Lost at sea,
rudderless. At the mercy of pitch and toss, clueless.
Given to fits of grandeur, despair, depression,
delusion... the fasting, no time (or inclination) to
eat. Fuelled by caffeine and nicotine. Afflicted by
the curse of the scribe- the blank page...tantalising,
mocking ..a murmur, a sentence...gone! But
wait..excitement, anticipation...it flows, as if by
another hand..
It is written! Euphoria, surprise (maybe even a
tear..)until next time- it starts again..could finally
be my best (or worst!)
Was it all really worth it?...
HELL YEAH .....

(End note)

Poetica

Thought I'd like to be a poet
So, off to class I went
Just got through the door, I did
Then out the door, I'm sent!
The teacher, she was not impressed
"You shall not waste my time!
You are a simple cretin,
You cannot make a rhyme!"
"But missus, I implore you
Just give me half a chance"
"Young man, I will ignore you,
I'll tell you in advance!"
What am I to do now?
She's shattered all my dreams
Career ended, not yet began
That's the way it seems...

Thought I'd like to be a poet
I still think I should
Started writing poems...
And some of them were good...

[poeta nascitur non fit]
Smudge 2019

Made in the USA
Las Vegas, NV
27 March 2022